MW01613172

YEAR 3

MENTOR

A FATHER'S GUIDE TO MENTORING HIS SON

Joy Church
P.O. Box 247
Mount Juliet, TN 37121
joychurch.net

Printed in the United States of America
Publisher's Cataloging-in-Publication data
Frease, Jim.
MENTOR: A Father's Guide to Mentoring his Son
-Year Three / Jim Frease
p. 132
ISBN 978-0-9983918-9-2
1. Motivational 2. Inspirational. 3. Christian Living.
First Edition
First Printing 2023

To my beloved son, Johnathan!

There is a 40-year old version of you,
sitting on the inside of you,
counting on you to choose wisely!
Continue to take these wisdom principles
and daily apply them to your life!

Eventually teach them to your own children.

I am proud of you; I believe in you;
I love you…and so does God!

CONTENTS

INTRODUCTION

I am an older father. When Anne (my wonderful wife) had John, I was 40 years old. (As a matter of fact, I just recently convinced my son that I am not his grandfather!) When Anne was pregnant with John, people would repeatedly tell me, "Pastor, they grow up fast." Well, we all have regrets in life, and I did not want raising my son to be one of them.

We have all heard horror stories of "pastor kids" and how so many of them were little "hellions". I did not want to "save the whole world" and have my son go to hell! Therefore, I wanted to do something very tangible so as to not have any regrets when it came to raising John.

I had a giant jug of protein powder to fuel my workouts and emptied it of all the protein powder. I then calculated how many weeks it would be from when John was born until he left for college and put that exact amount of rocks in the big jar. Then for the last 18 years, every single Saturday morning, I have taken out one rock at a time and prayed various prayers that have gone something like this: "Father, help me to make my time with John count," "Father, help me to have no regrets as a dad," "Father, give me wisdom on how to mentor my son."

Over the years, I have watched those rocks slowly diminish. As I write this, there are but a few rocks left in the jar and a few small tears in my eyes. However they are not tears of regret...but tears of love!

As a result of those prayers, when John was about ten years old, I sensed God leading me to spend a structured and intentional time with John on a weekly basis. We decided to call it "Men's Night." For us, this was Thursday evenings. My beautiful wife leads the praise and worship at our church and rehearsal for her team has been on Thursdays. My son and I would usually go to some local sandwich shop and find a table in the back corner (when you are the pastor of a large church you can be easily recognized, and I wanted to devote this time to investing solely into my son).

We would purchase our sandwiches, sit down and the first part of our conversation was always relational, nothing heavy. I simply asked John questions about his day and the various things going on in his life. I intentionally kept it lighthearted and fun and incorporated my sense of humor. Many times, the shortest distance between any two people can be a sense of humor!

After we ate, I always had one wisdom principle (I call them "Pastor Jim Nuggets") that I shared with him. Particularly when John was young I would keep our impartation time relatively short.

(Remember: Information can be shared from afar but impartation can only be done up close.) A child's retention span is only as good as his attention span!

After I shared the principle, I would try to share a personal story that would augment the teaching principle. I simply borrowed that teaching method from our Lord Jesus Christ when He taught in parables. The Greek word translated for the word "parable" is *parabole*. It is a Greek compound word derived from *para* which means "to come along side" and *bole* which means "to throw down." Put those two Greek words together and the word "parable" means "to come along side and throw down." Jesus would come alongside a teaching principle and throw down a story that would augment the teaching.

Once I thought John was comprehending the principle, I would say, "Ok John, now re-teach me." I would then let him teach me in one or two sentences what I just taught him. I simply wanted to make sure John was comprehending what I taught him, as the teacher has not truly taught until the student has truly learned!

I would always have John carry with him his "Men's Night" notebook. I would have him write down the wisdom nugget in this notebook. I taught him to treasure this notebook and take care of it... knowing that it could be a treasured source of wisdom for the rest of his life and for his future family!

I never intended "Men's Night" to eventually become a book, but a number of years ago, Pastor Ben Pierce, a dear spiritual son in the faith, suggested this. He said, "Pastor Jim, you should turn this into a book as it will help thousands of fathers and their sons." Now, Pastor Ben has a little boy, and after I give my son Johnathan the first copy, Pastor Ben and his son will get the second copy!

As I look back over my son's "Men's Night" notebook, it is touching to see how even his spelling and handwriting transforms from a ten year old boy to an 18 year old young man! When my son was about 12 or 13, my mentoring method began to evolve. Rather than just teaching him, I began to ask him questions. I learned this principle from Luke 2:46-47. Here these powerful verses reveal to us how Jesus learned when he was just 12 years old: "Now so it was that after three days they found Him in the temple [this should make all of us parents feel so much better about our parenting skills as Mary and Joseph LOST Jesus for <u>three days</u>...yet Jesus turned out pretty good!], sitting in the midst of the teachers both <u>listening</u> to them and <u>asking</u> <u>them</u> <u>questions</u>. And all who heard Him were astonished at His <u>understanding</u> and answers."

As your son gets into the 12 to teenage category, some things begin to switch internally in him. Every young Christian teen will go through a transition from the relationship <u>you</u> have with the Lord to the relationship he has with the Lord. It is a process that all teenage believers go through. Expect a few bumpy roads during this transitional time. It's part of the process. Your son is transitioning from living vicariously through your relationship with God to his own.

In years 13-14, John went through a bit of a rebellious period. Nothing major, but we still had to work through some things. However we both kept our hearts tender towards God and each other and pressed on in our Men's Nights together. Particularly during this time, I discovered that asking John questions was instrumental in him

developing his own relationship with God. When John was younger, I would tell him what to think from a biblical perspective. As a teen, he needed to come to his own conclusions as he was developing his own walk with God. This had to be more than just "Daddy said so," therefore it must be true. The Bible tells us, "Great is the peace of our children, they will be taught of the Lord" (Isaiah 54:13).

Fathers, children's pastors, youth pastors, and pastors are all instruments that God uses to teach us, but eventually our children must be taught of the Lord. In the kingdom of God, there are no grandchildren, only sons and daughters. In other words, our teenagers must develop **their own** life-giving relationship with God. It's true, nobody can talk you into anything like **you** can!

When I would ask John questions, it forced him to think for himself. Many times, he would come to the wrong conclusions. If he did, I would gently steer him back to the biblical principle until understanding occurred.

In all transparency, there were times when I would be a bit impatient when comprehension came too slowly or even incorrectly. If I was impatient, I would simply ask John to forgive me and ask God to help me be a better parent.

I always wanted to keep open lines of dialogue. I wanted John to be able to come to me with anything, even difficult things. As John traversed into the teenage years, I would ask him open and honest questions about lust, masturbation, pornography, and sex. These are not always easy to navigate, but they are challenges every young man and every man faces! The key to this working with you and your son is two-fold:

FIRST, you must develop a relationship with him that is open, communicative, and loving from when he is a young child. If you have not cultivated the trust that comes from years of loving investments into your son when he is young, it will not go over well when you read a book like this one and with no investments in relational capital suddenly ask your teenage boy, "So son...how's it going with that whole pornography thing?"

All relationships consist of caring and candor. Care without candor leads to a dysfunctional relationship. Candor without care leads to a distant relationship. Care balanced with candor leads to a developing relationship. You must deposit enough "care coins" into the relational bucket or your candor with your teen will not be sustained.

SECOND, if your son comes to you (as you hopefully have invited him to do) with some honest but uncomfortable information, **don't** **freak** **out**! If you do, you will inadvertently teach him to take all his private information to his friends who are just as clueless as he is on how to navigate these difficult waters! To this day, my son and I have an open, honest relationship—one in which the caring can sustain the candor!

Dads, I don't want to create some utopian and unattainable picture in your mind. My 18-year old son John is not Billy Graham and neither is his 59-year old father! Just like his dad (and just like you), my son is still a work in progress. He will have to continue to apply all I have imparted into him as he navigates living on his own, marriage, children, and his God-given destiny. However, he has his own walk with God, Biblical and personal convictions, and he works part-time with us in ministry!

Here are **3 WAYS** to learn in life:

1. FROM YOUR OWN MISTAKES - THAT IS GOOD

2. FROM ANOTHER'S MISTAKES - THAT IS BETTER

3. FROM ANOTHER'S SUCCESSES - THAT IS BEST

Your son needs a mentor! Mentors are shortcuts. Remember Dads...the **power** of the **protégé** is always determined by the **might** of the **mentor**!

A MENTOR'S MANUAL
How to Use this Book

In Jeremiah 3:15, the Bible tells us, "And I will give you shepherds according to My heart, who will feed you with knowledge and understanding." Notice the two words "knowledge and understanding." Knowledge is the "what" but understanding is the "how". Over decades of being in the ministry, I have always endeavored not just to teach the people I serve what to do, but *how* to do it. If I just tell you dads the *what*: "You need to mentor your son" without the *how* to practically do it, you will be frustrated and not motivated. However, if I can tell you the *what* with the *how* along with it, you will not be frustrated, but motivated.

OK Dads, here is how to practically use this book. It took me approximately eight years of "Men's Nights" to mentor my son. I want to condense this down to three years of mentoring material just for you. This book is YEAR THREE.

In the following pages I have provided for you three essentials to mentor your son:

1 BIBLICAL BASIS
I have provided the Biblical basis for every wisdom principle contained within this book. Why live in a "grey" world when you have a "black and white" Bible?

2 MENTOR MESSAGE
This is the "Pastor Jim Nugget" that you want to share with your son. Have him write it down in his own notebook and teach him to treasure it. What you prize, you will prioritize.

3 SON STANDARD
This is the key "takeaway" you want your son to understand as you mentor him. Understanding releases submission.

BIBLICAL BASIS

"THEREFORE, PUTTING AWAY LYING, LET EACH ONE OF YOU SPEAK TRUTH WITH HIS NEIGHBOR FOR WE ARE MEMBERS OF ONE ANOTHER."

- EPHESIANS 4:25

TRUTH
TRUTH
TRUTH
TRUTH
TRUTH
TRUTH
TRUTH

MENTOR MESSAGE

TELL THE TRUTH.
TELL IT EARLY.
TELL IT YOURSELF.
TELL IT ALL.

SON STANDARD

PEOPLE WHO HAVE NOTHING TO HIDE

HIDE NOTHING

9

Now, may I encourage you to find a little inexpensive restaurant where you can have a little privacy and get away with your son. If it's not in your budget, pack a dinner and go to a park. Use your imagination! Be creative! Make it special! Be consistent!

Mark the time on your calendar and prioritize it. Let almost nothing come between you and Men's Night with your son. Value is always determined by the price that is paid.

Dads, if you pay the price to prioritize this encounter with your son, your son will see his true value!

May I also suggest you find a big jar, and no matter how old your son is, determine how many rocks you should place in that jar until he goes to college.

It is my prayer when you get down to those last few rocks like I have…you will have a tear in your eye but no regret in your heart as you have mentored your son!

BIBLICAL BASIS

"THEREFORE DO NOT BE **UNWISE**, BUT UNDERSTAND WHAT THE **WILL OF THE LORD IS**"

EPHESIANS 5:17

MENTOR MESSAGE

DON'T ASK YOURSELF, "WHAT'S WRONG WITH THAT?"

ASK YOURSELF, "**WHAT'S THE WISE THING TO DO?**"

THE FIRST QUESTION DETERMINES HOW LOW YOU CAN GO.

THE SECOND QUESTION DETERMINES HOW HIGH YOU CAN REACH.

JUST BECAUSE IT'S NOT WRONG DOES NOT MAKE IT *Wise!*

BIBLICAL BASIS

"THE RIGHTEOUS SHOULD CHOOSE HIS FRIENDS **CAREFULLY**, FOR THE WAY OF THE WICKED LEADS THEM ASTRAY."

Proverbs 12:26

MENTOR MESSAGE

LIFE IS NOT ABOUT **INTENTIONS**, IT IS ABOUT **DIRECTIONS**.

LEARN TO EVALUATE RELATIONSHIPS NOT BASED ON WHERE YOU ARE BUT **WHERE YOU WANT TO GO.**

WHEN YOU CHOOSE YOUR CONNECTIONS,

YOU CHOOSE THEIR DIRECTIONS.

BIBLICAL BASIS

HE WHO WALKS WITH WISE MEN WILL BE WISE, BUT THE COMPANION OF FOOLS WILL BE DESTROYED.
- PROVERBS 13:20

MENTOR MESSAGE

RIGHT VOICES, RIGHT CHOICES. WRONG VOICES, WRONG CHOICES.

RIGHT CONNECTIONS, RIGHT DIRECTIONS. WRONG CONNECTIONS, WRONG DIRECTIONS.

SON STANDARD

FRIENDS ARE CONTAGIOUS

BIBLICAL BASIS

FINALLY, BRETHREN, WHATEVER THINGS ARE TRUE, WHATEVER THINGS ARE NOBLE, WHATEVER THINGS ARE JUST, WHATEVER THINGS ARE PURE, WHATEVER THINGS ARE LOVELY, WHATEVER THINGS ARE OF GOOD REPORT, IF THERE IS ANY VIRTUE AND IF THERE IS ANYTHING PRAISEWORTHY — MEDITATE ON THESE THINGS.

- PHILIPPIANS 4:8

MENTOR MESSAGE

LIFE IS NOT AS BAD AS YOU THINK IT IS.
LIFE IS AS BAD AS YOU THINK IT IS.

SON STANDARD

WHAT YOU CONTINUALLY MIND,
YOU'LL EVENTUALLY FIND.

Biblical Basis

"BEHOLD, I STAND AT
THE DOOR AND KNOCK.
IF ANYONE HEARS MY VOICE
AND OPENS THE DOOR,
I WILL COME IN TO HIM
AND DINE WITH HIM,
AND HE WITH ME."

– Revelation 3:20

Mentor Message

YOU'LL NEVER GET
THE BEST OF GOD
WHEN YOU ONLY GIVE HIM
HALF OF YOU.

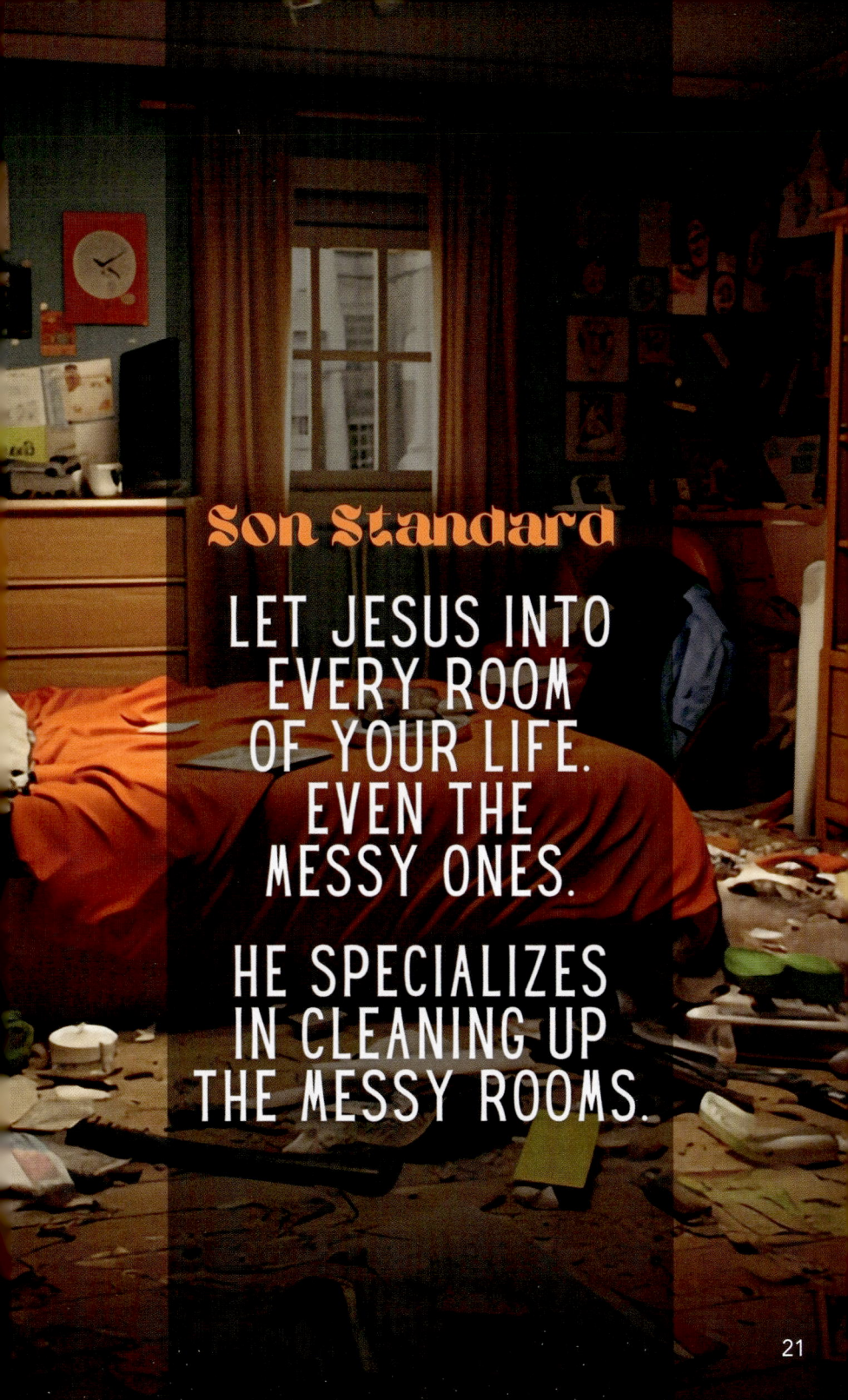

Son Standard

LET JESUS INTO
EVERY ROOM
OF YOUR LIFE.
EVEN THE
MESSY ONES.

HE SPECIALIZES
IN CLEANING UP
THE MESSY ROOMS.

"FOR THOSE WHO LIVE ACCORDING TO THE FLESH SET THEIR MINDS ON THE THINGS OF THE FLESH, BUT THOSE WHO LIVE ACCORDING TO THE SPIRIT, THE THINGS OF THE SPIRIT.
FOR TO BE CARNALLY MINDED IS DEATH, BUT TO BE SPIRITUALLY MINDED IS LIFE AND PEACE."

– ROMANS 8:5-6

Mentor Message

IF YOU THINK THE WAY YOU USED TO THINK... YOU'LL DO THE THINGS YOU USED TO DO.

Son Standard

SOMETIMES WE NEED A CHECK-UP FROM THE NECK UP.

LET'S GET RID OF STINKIN' THINKIN' WITH THE WORD OF THE LIVING GOD!

BIBLICAL BASIS

"THE GLORY OF YOUNG MEN IS THEIR STRENGTH, AND THE SPLENDOR OF OLD MEN IS THEIR GRAY HEAD."

Proverbs 20:29

MENTOR MESSAGE

IS THE DECISION **I AM MAKING TODAY** COMPATIBLE WITH THE STORY I WANT TO TELL **AT THE END OF MY LIFE?**

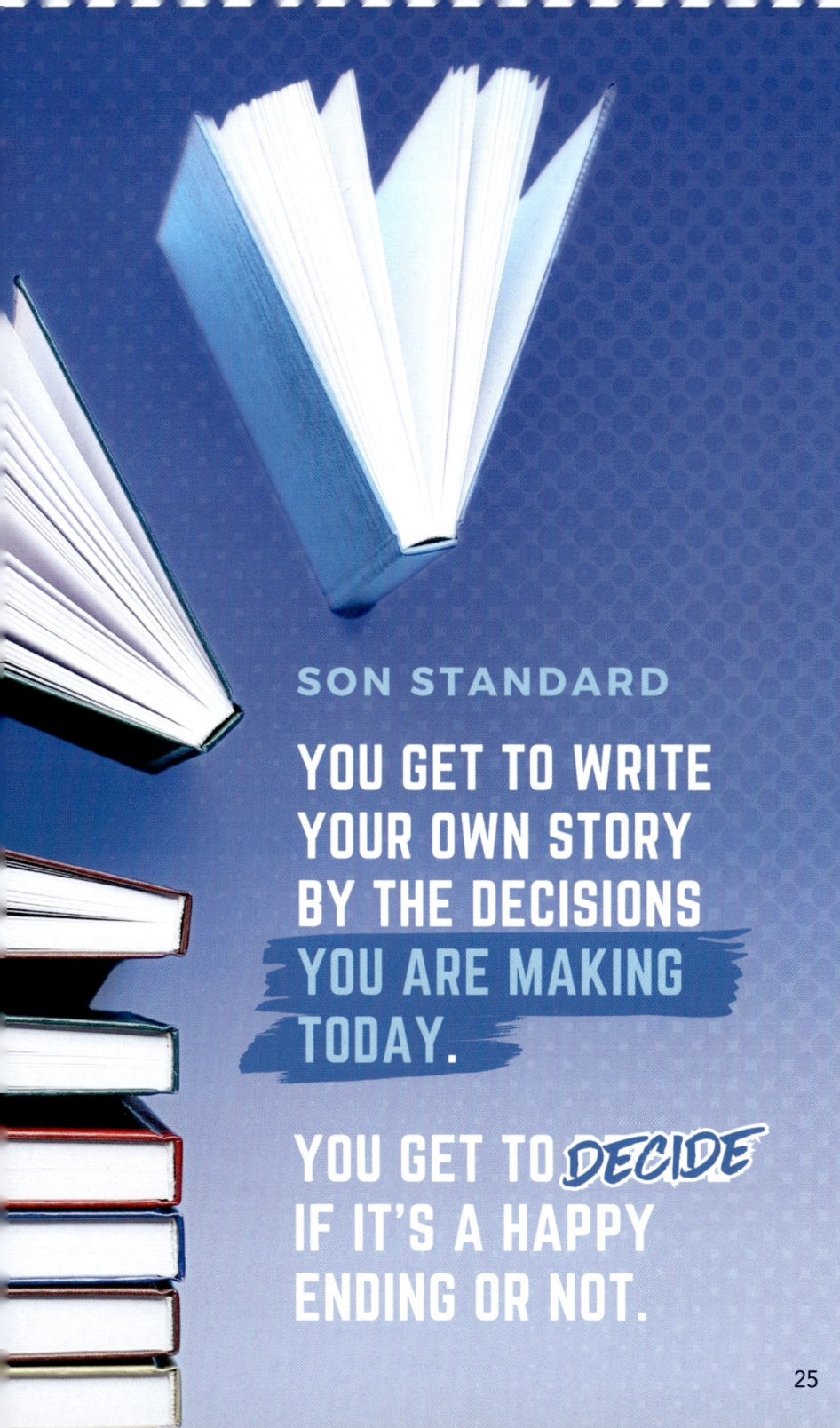

YOU GET TO WRITE YOUR OWN STORY BY THE DECISIONS YOU ARE MAKING TODAY.

YOU GET TO *DECIDE* IF IT'S A HAPPY ENDING OR NOT.

BIBLICAL BASIS

"Do not love the world or the things in the world. If anyone loves the world, the love of the Father is not in him. For all that is in the world – the lust of the flesh, the lust of the eyes, and the pride of life – is not of the Father but is of the world. And the world is passing away, and the lust of it; but he who does the will of God abides forever."

I JOHN 2:15-17

MENTOR MESSAGE

**If you take in
more of the world
than you do of the Word
. . . your discouragement
is self-inflicted.**

WHAT GETS YOUR ATTENTION GETS YOU!

SON STANDARD

27

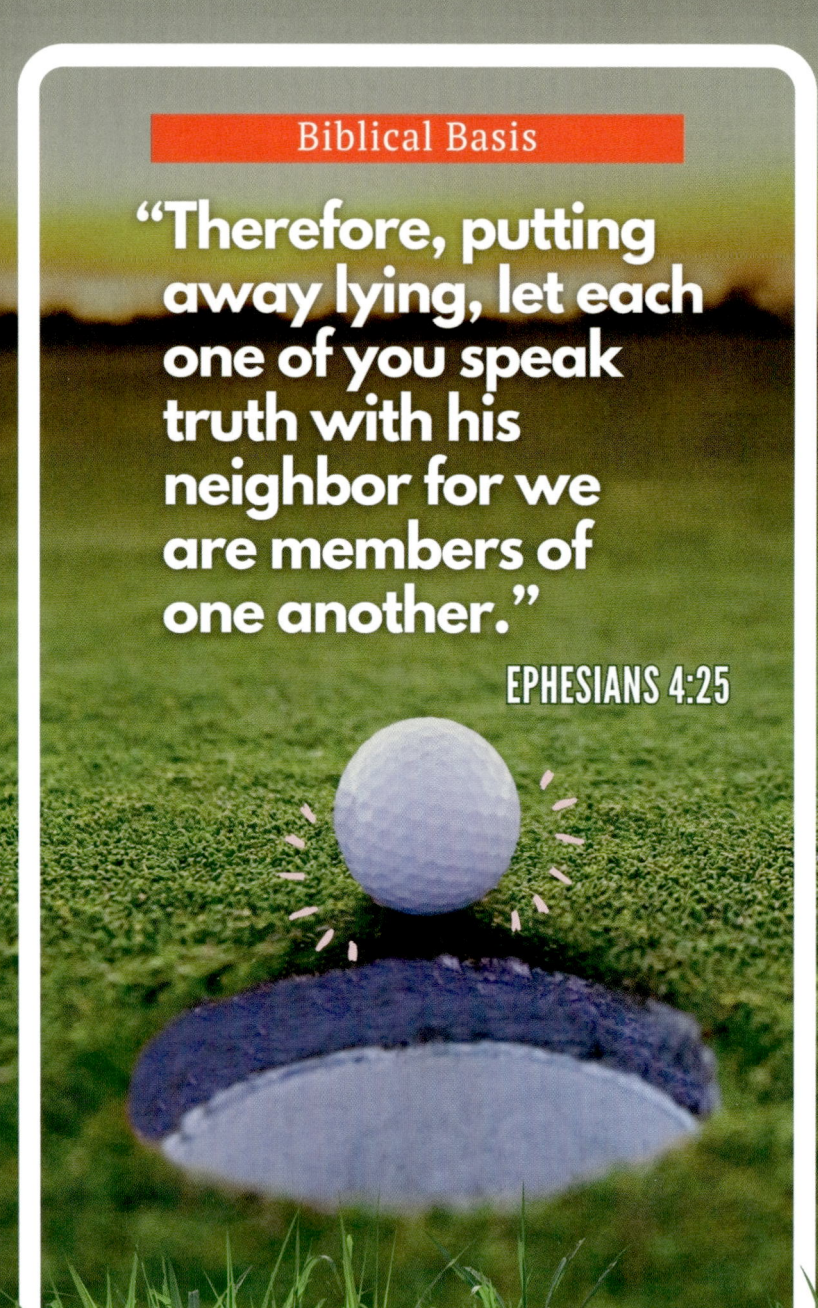

Biblical Basis

"Therefore, putting away lying, let each one of you speak truth with his neighbor for we are members of one another."

EPHESIANS 4:25

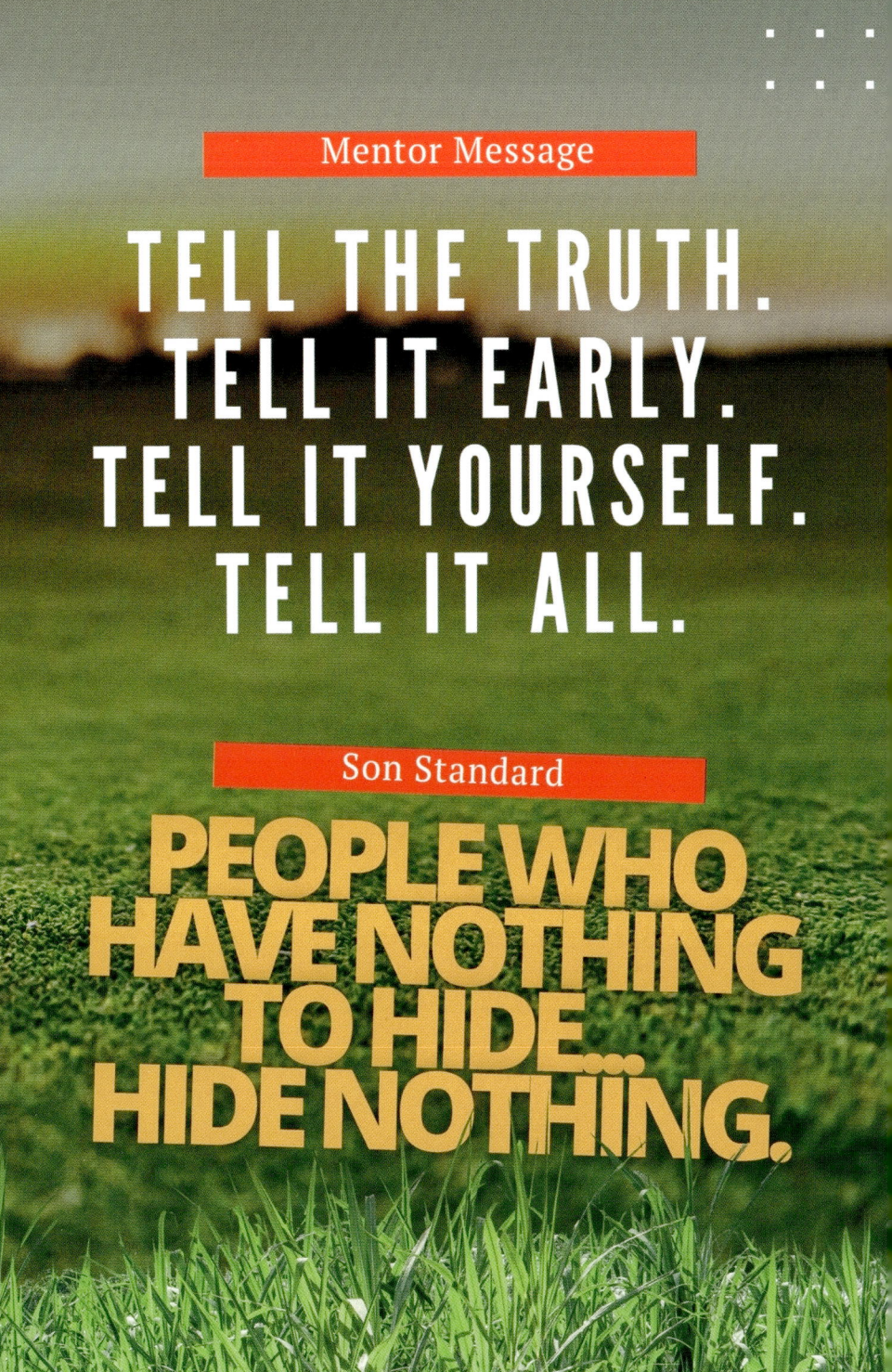

Mentor Message

TELL THE TRUTH. TELL IT EARLY. TELL IT YOURSELF. TELL IT ALL.

Son Standard

PEOPLE WHO HAVE NOTHING TO HIDE... HIDE NOTHING.

29

BIBLICAL BASIS

"THEN THE SPIRIT OF THE LORD WILL COME UPON YOU, AND YOU WILL PROPHESY WITH THEM AND BE TURNED INTO ANOTHER MAN."

I SAMUEL 10:6

MENTOR MESSAGE

PEOPLE KNOW EVERYTHING YOU HAVE BEEN. GOD KNOWS EVERYTHING YOU COULD BE.

Son Standard

YOU ARE "TWO PEOPLE":
WHO YOU ARE AND
WHO YOU CAN BE.

TAKE THE WORD OF GOD
AND RENEW YOUR MIND
AND BECOME ALL GOD
WANTS YOU TO BE!

02:20   - 00:58

BIBLICAL BASIS

"THEREFORE, IF ANYONE
IS IN CHRIST,
HE IS A NEW CREATION;
OLD THINGS HAVE PASSED AWAY;
BEHOLD, ALL THINGS
HAVE BECOME NEW."

2 CORINTHIANS 5:17

MENTOR MESSAGE

LET YOUR PAST REMIND YOU... DON'T LET YOUR PAST DEFINE YOU.

SON STANDARD

LEARN FROM PAST MISTAKES OR
YOU ARE DOOMED TO REPEAT THEM.
HOWEVER DON'T LET
WHAT YOU DID DEFINE YOU...
YOU ARE SO MUCH MORE THAN THAT!

WEEK 12

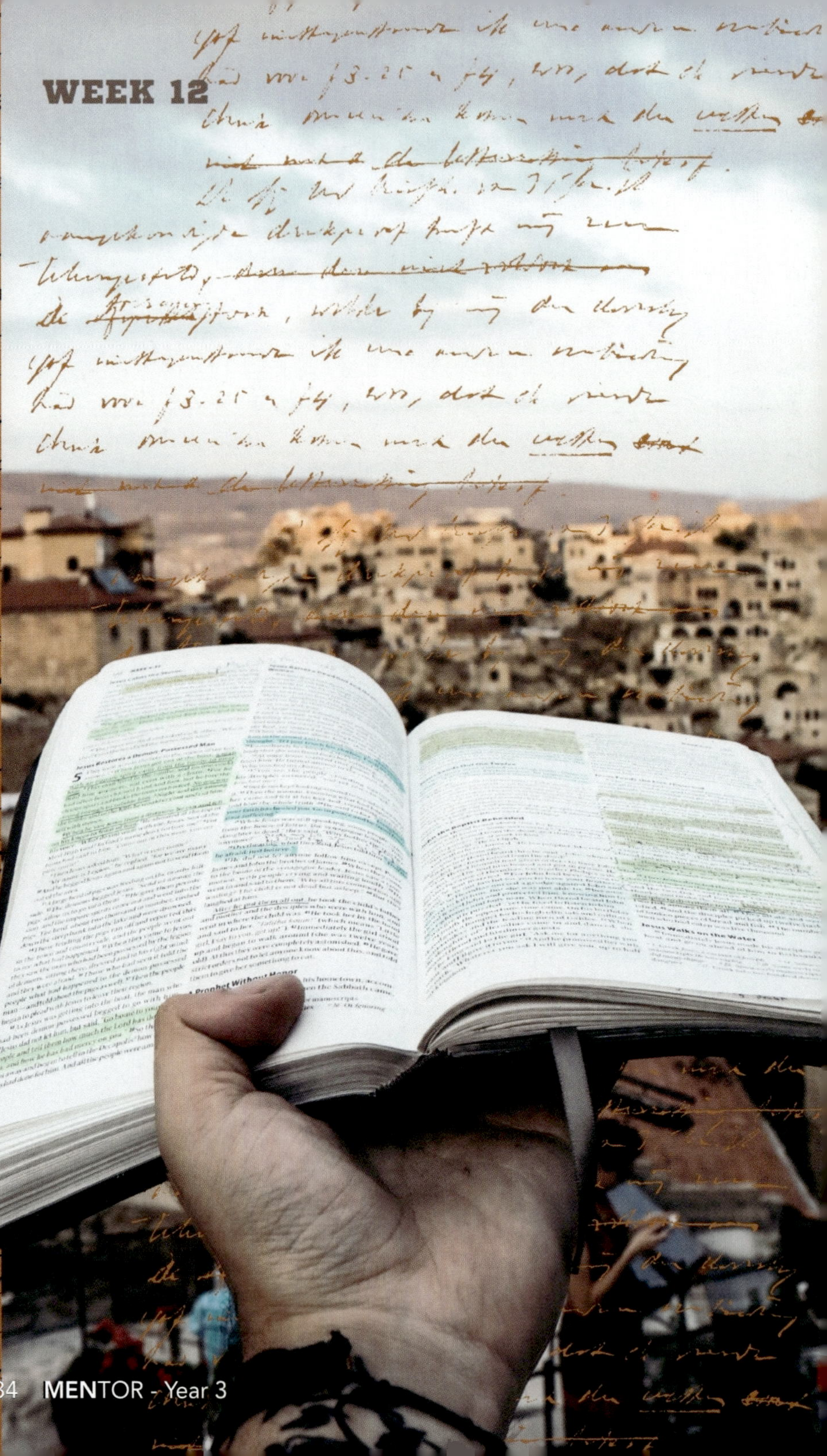

Biblical Basis

"But without faith it is impossible to please Him, for he who comes to God must believe that He is, and that He is a rewarder of those who diligently seek Him."

Hebrews 11:6

Mentor Message

RELIGION LIKES WHO JESUS <u>WAS</u>.

Relationship LIKES WHO JESUS <u>IS</u>.

Son Standard

Stay current on your relationship with Jesus on a daily basis.

BIBLICAL BASIS

"FOR THE LOVE OF MONEY IS A ROOT OF ALL KINDS OF EVIL, FOR WHICH SOME HAVE STRAYED FROM THE FAITH IN THEIR GREEDINESS, AND PIERCED THEMSELVES THROUGH WITH MANY SORROWS."

– 1 Timothy 6:10

SON STANDARD

MONEY IN AND OF ITSELF IS AMORAL.

WHAT WE DO WITH IT ASSIGNS MORALITY TO IT.

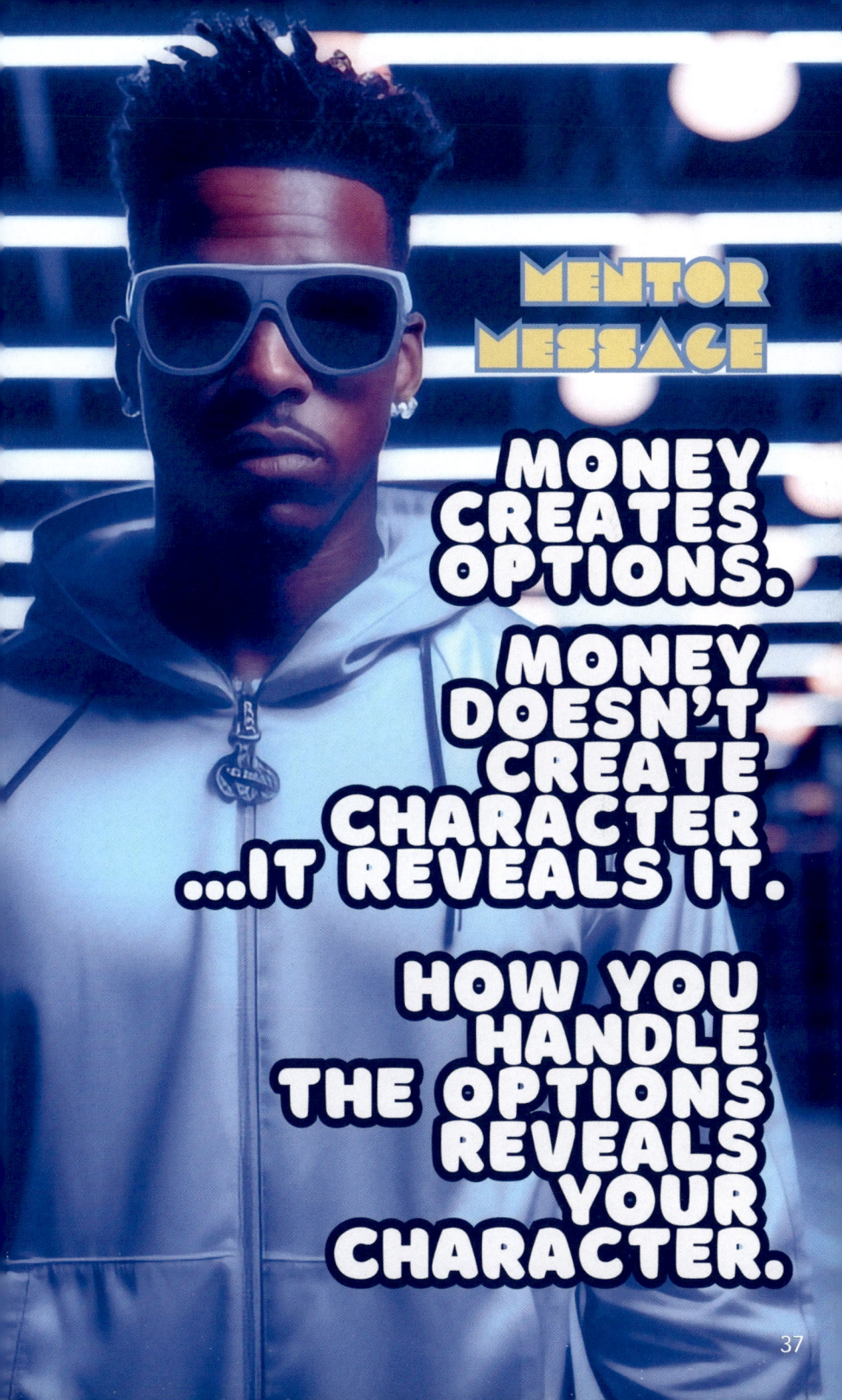

**MONEY
CREATES
OPTIONS.**

**MONEY
DOESN'T
CREATE
CHARACTER
...IT REVEALS IT.**

**HOW YOU
HANDLE
THE OPTIONS
REVEALS
YOUR
CHARACTER.**

BIBLICAL BASIS

"AND THE YOUNGER OF THEM SAID TO HIS FATHER, 'FATHER, GIVE ME THE PORTION OF GOODS THAT FALLS TO ME.' SO HE DIVIDED TO THEM HIS LIVELIHOOD. AND I AM NO LONGER WORTHY TO BE CALLED YOUR SON. MAKE ME LIKE ONE OF YOUR HIRED SERVANTS."

- LUKE 15:12,19

MENTOR MESSAGE

THE PRODIGAL SON SAID, "GIVE ME" BEFORE HE SAID "MAKE ME."

IF HE WOULD HAVE SAID "MAKE ME" BEFORE HE SAID "GIVE ME"...

HE WOULDN'T HAVE WASTED HIS INHERITANCE.

SON STANDARD

GREAT
CHARACTER
SUSTAINS
GREAT
CALLING

BIBLICAL BASIS

"Not that I speak in regard to need, for I have learned in whatever state I am, to be content:"

- PHILIPPIANS 4:11

MENTOR MESSAGE

NEVER LET THE BLESSINGS YOU WANT ROB YOU OF THE BLESSINGS THAT YOU HAVE

SON STANDARD

THE BIBLE TEACHES YOU A PERFECT BALANCE BETWEEN CONTENTMENT WITH WHAT YOU HAVE NOW AND DESIRE FOR MORE TOMORROW.

YOU'RE NOT WHERE YOU WANT TO BE, BUT THANK GOD YOU'RE NOT WHERE YOU USED TO BE!

● ● ● ● ● ● ● ● ● ● ● ●

CELEBRATE PROGRESS!

BIBLICAL BASIS

" *and your zeal hath provoked very many.* "

2 corinthians 9:2-b kjv

MENTOR MESSAGE

there are two kinds of people in life:

those who let their environment influence their enthusiasm

------ and ------

those who let their enthusiasm influence their environment.

Son Standard

DON'T CONFORM TO
"ROOM TEMPERATURE".
BE A THERMOSTAT...
NOT A THERMOMETER!

BIBLICAL BASIS

"And whoever compels you to go one mile, go with him two."

MATTHEW 5:41

mentor message

NO ONE STANDS IN LINE FOR "AVERAGE".

son standard

BE A MAN OF EXCELLENCE. THERE IS VERY LITTLE TRAFFIC ON THE "EXTRA MILE".

BIBLICAL BASIS

"Then He said to them all,
'If anyone desires
to come after Me,
let him deny himself, and
take up his cross daily,
and follow Me".

Luke 9:23

MENTOR MESSAGE

There is no success without sacrifice. Quit praying for success and start participating **in sacrifice.**

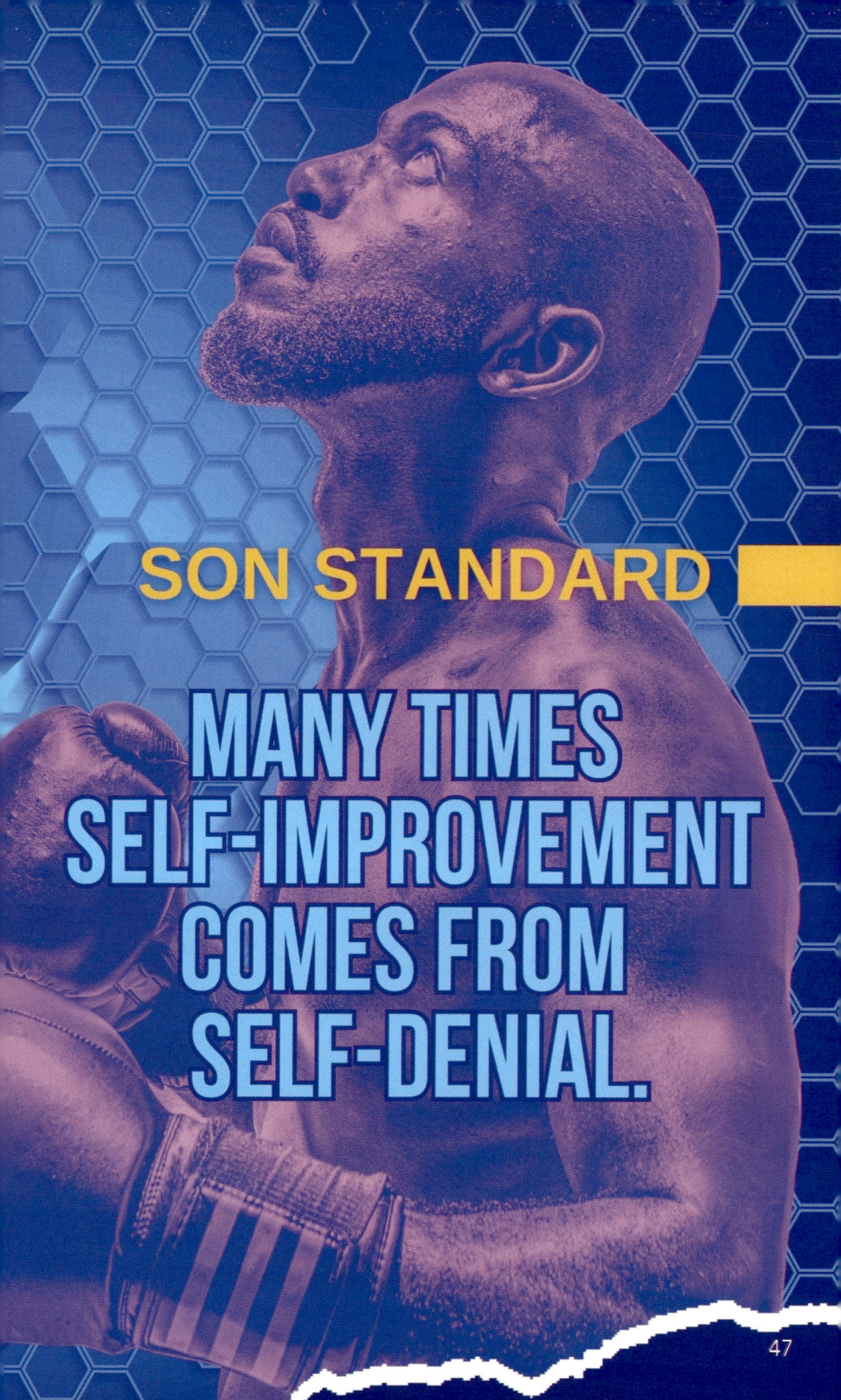

SON STANDARD

MANY TIMES SELF-IMPROVEMENT COMES FROM SELF-DENIAL.

47

BIBLICAL
BASIS

"And whatever
you do,
do it heartily,
as to the Lord
and not to men,"
- *Colossians 3:23*

MENTOR
MESSAGE

If you want to be successful:

1 SOLVE PROBLEMS

2 GO THE EXTRA MILE

3 HAVE A STELLAR ATTITUDE

SON
STANDARD

IF YOU DO THESE
THREE THINGS,
YOU WILL BRING

GLORY TO GOD

AND BE

PROMOTED BY MAN

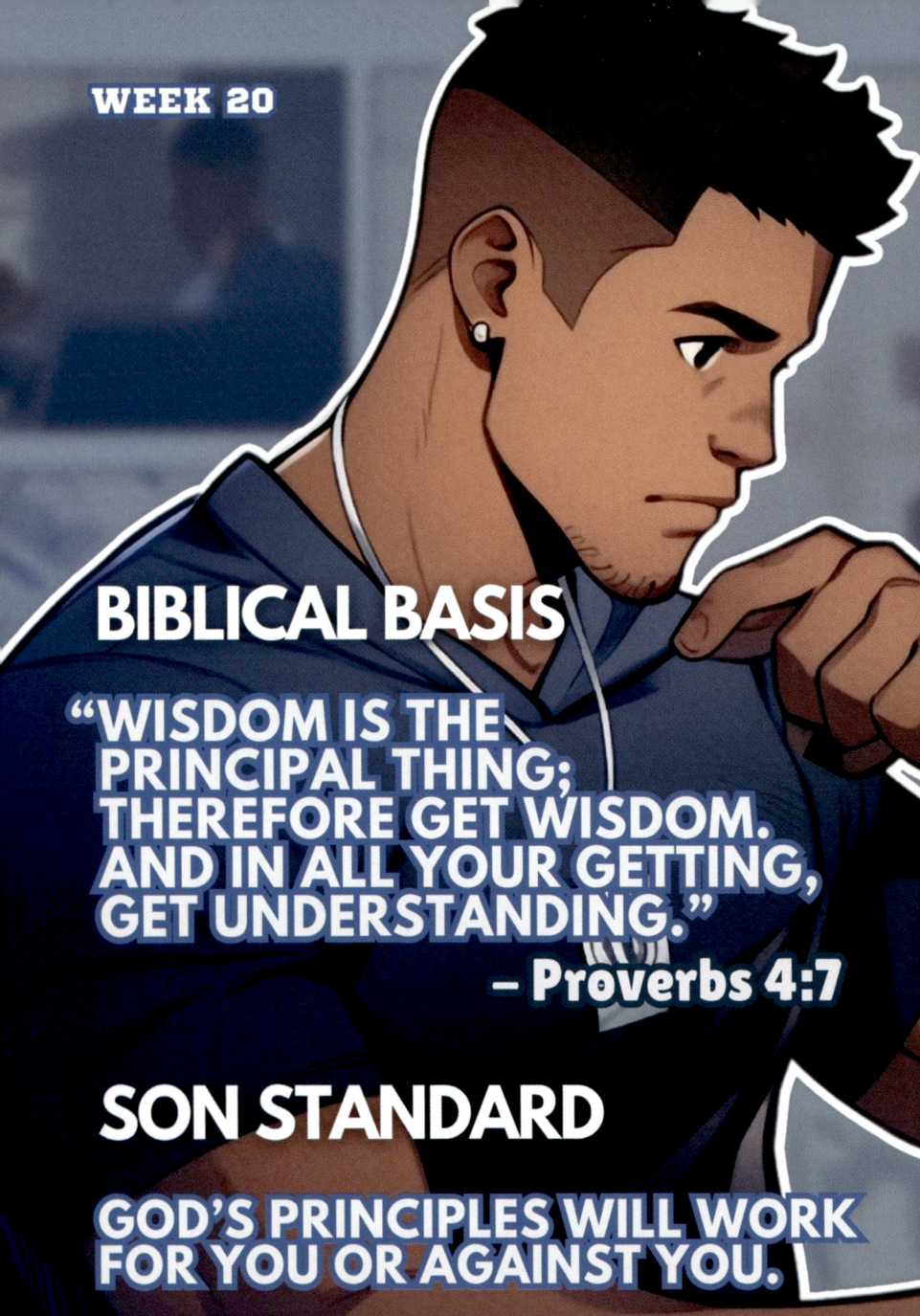

BIBLICAL BASIS

"WISDOM IS THE PRINCIPAL THING; THEREFORE GET WISDOM. AND IN ALL YOUR GETTING, GET UNDERSTANDING."

– Proverbs 4:7

SON STANDARD

GOD'S PRINCIPLES WILL WORK FOR YOU OR AGAINST YOU.

HIS PRINCIPLES ARE FOUND IN HIS WORD!

MENTOR MESSAGE

THERE IS A DIFFERENCE BETWEEN KNOWING THE PERSON OF JESUS AND KNOWING THE PRINCIPLES OF JESUS.

YOU CAN KNOW THE PERSON OF JESUS AND BE ON YOUR WAY TO HEAVEN WHILE EXPERIENCING HELL ON EARTH.

IF YOU KNOW THE PRINCIPLES OF JESUS YOU CAN EXPERIENCE A LITTLE BIT OF HEAVEN ON EARTH!

BIBLICAL BASIS

"Then Jesus said to those Jews who believed Him, 'If you abide in My word, you are My disciples indeed. And you shall know the truth, and the truth shall make you free." - John 8:31-32

MENTOR MESSAGE

There is a difference between a convert and a disciple. Converts transfer their trust from themselves to Jesus for eternal life. Disciples transfer trust from themselves to the Word of God for abundant life.

Converts choose Heaven over hell.

Disciples choose Heaven on earth.

SON STANDARD

Continue in His Word! It's not the truth I know that will make you free... it's the truth **YOU** know that will make you free!

"THEREFORE, SINCE ALL THESE THINGS WILL BE DISSOLVED, WHAT MANNER OF PERSONS OUGHT YOU TO BE IN HOLY CONDUCT AND GODLINESS."

2 Peter: 3:11

WHEN WE RECOGNIZE TOMORROW MATTERS, IT WILL CHANGE THE WAY WE LIVE TODAY.

son standard

LEARN TO LIVE YOUR LIFE IN LIGHT OF ETERNITY.

BIBLICAL BASIS
BIBLICAL BASIS
BIBLICAL BASIS
BIBLICAL BASIS
BIBLICAL BASIS
BIBLICAL BASIS
BIBLICAL BASIS
BIBLICAL BASIS
BIBLICAL BASIS
BIBLICAL BASIS
BIBLICAL BASIS
BIBLICAL BASIS
BIBLICAL BASIS
BIBLICAL BASIS
BIBLICAL BASIS
BIBLICAL BASIS

"FOR A GREAT AND EFFECTIVE DOOR HAS OPENED TO ME, AND THERE ARE MANY ADVERSARIES."

- I CORINTHIANS 16:9

MENTOR MESSAGE
MENTOR MESSAGE
MENTOR MESSAGE
MENTOR MESSAGE
MENTOR MESSAGE
MENTOR MESSAGE
MENTOR MESSAGE
MENTOR MESSAGE
MENTOR MESSAGE

YOU DON'T *GO* INTO AN OPPORTUNITY...YOU *GROW* INTO AN OPPORTUNITY.

SON STANDARD
SON STANDARD
SON STANDARD
SON STANDARD
SON STANDARD
SON STANDARD
SON STANDARD
SON STANDARD

IT IS AMAZING HOW DOORS OF OPPORTUNITY OPEN... WHEN YOU *GROW* INTO THEM.

Biblical Basis

"For as he thinks in his heart, so is he."

PROVERBS 23:7

Mentor Message

If you meet a jerk in the morning, you simply met a jerk. If you meet jerks all day long . . . you are the jerk!

Son Standard

We tend to see in others what we are dealing with ourselves. Wherever you go . . . there you are!

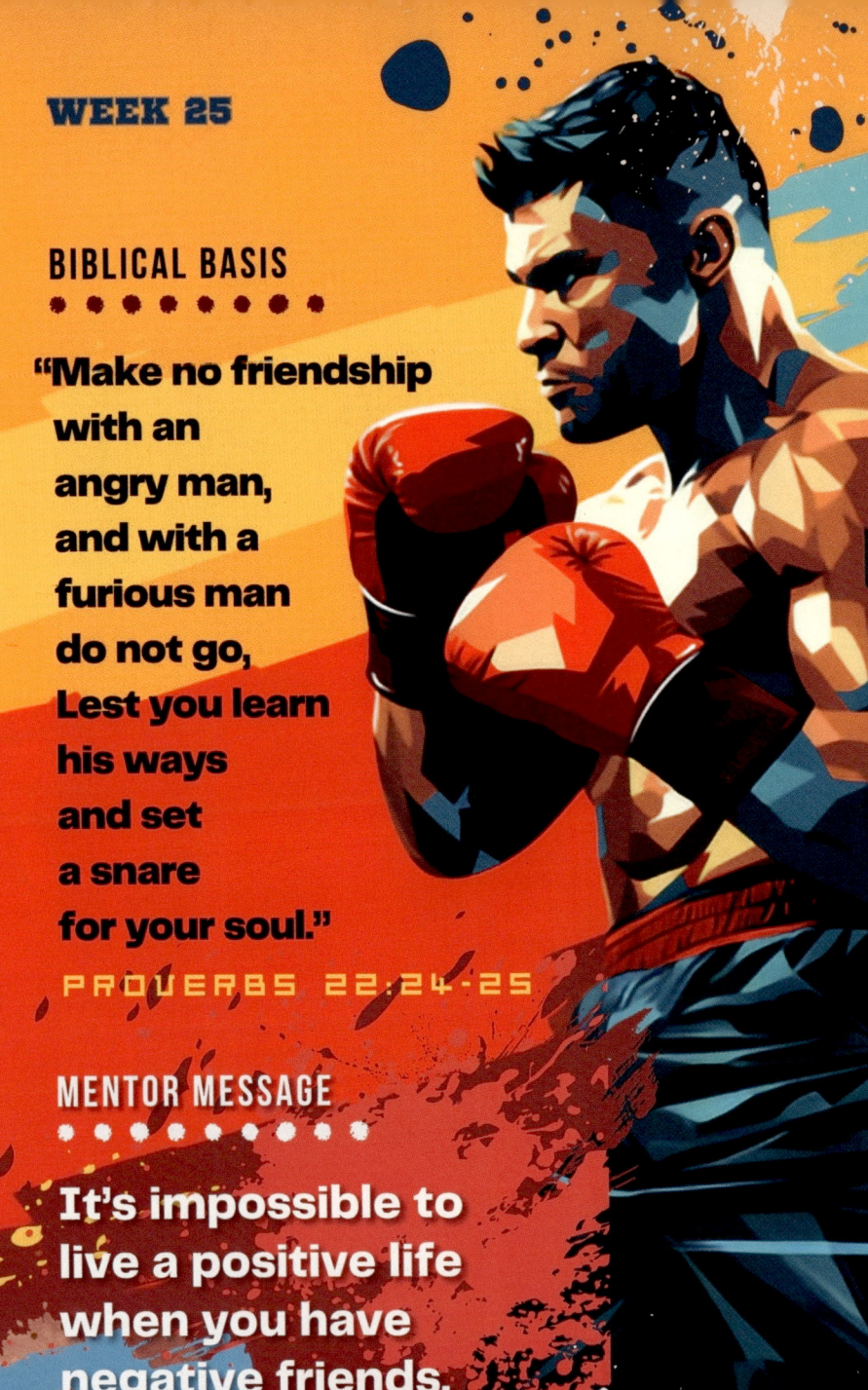

BIBLICAL BASIS

• • • • • • • •

"Make no friendship with an angry man, and with a furious man do not go, Lest you learn his ways and set a snare for your soul."

PROVERBS 22:24-25

MENTOR MESSAGE

• • • • • • • • •

It's impossible to live a positive life when you have negative friends.

SON STANDARD

SHOW ME YOUR
THREE CLOSEST FRIENDS
AND I WILL SHOW YOU...
YOU!

SHOW ME YOUR
THREE CLOSEST FRIENDS
AND I WILL SHOW YOU
YOUR FUTURE!

biblical basis

"Do not be deceived:
Evil company
corrupts
good habits."
- *I Corinthians 15:33*

mentor message

Your
weakest friend
is the devil's
strongest
entry point.

son standard

MAKE SURE YOUR CLOSEST FRIENDS

HAVE A STRONG RELATIONSHIP WITH GOD!

biblical basis

"Because they do not change,
therefore they do not fear God."
Psalm 55:19b

mentor message

It's the little changes
that no one sees,
that creates the
big things everyone wants.

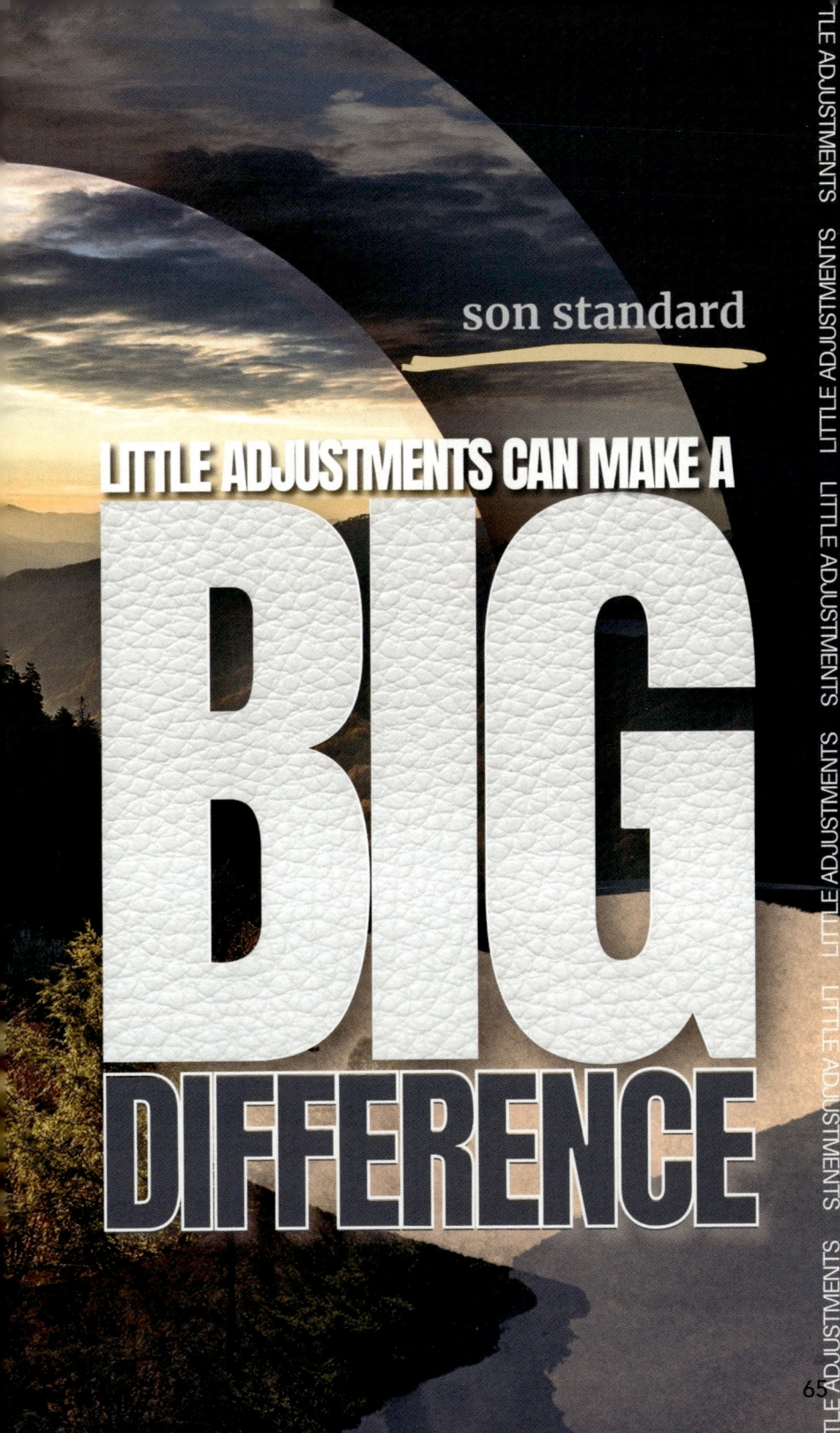

son standard

LITTLE ADJUSTMENTS CAN MAKE A

BIG

DIFFERENCE

B "Moreover if your brother sins against you, go and tell him his fault between you and him alone. If he hears you, you have gained your brother."

Matthew 18:15

M Never share a problem with someone who doesn't have the ability to solve it.

When you go <u>UP</u> with a problem, you are looking for a solution to the problem.

When you go <u>DOWN</u> with a problem, you are looking to perpetuate the problem.

In life, you will be remembered by the problems that you solved or the problems you created. Don't just be a problem seer...

BE A PROBLEM SOLVER.

BIBLICAL BASIS

"But put on the Lord Jesus Christ, and make no provision for the flesh, to fulfill its lusts."

ROMANS 13:14

MENTOR MESSAGE

TODAY'S PREVENTION STOPS TOMORROW'S TEMPTATION.

SON STANDARD

You can't win from a losing position.

Biblical Basis

"Let no one seek his own, but each one the other's well-being."

1 Corinthians 10:24

Mentor Message

You can't be a selfish person and live a significant life.

Son Standard

In Proverbs 22:9
& Proverbs 11:25,
the Bible talks about
a "generous eye" and
a "generous soul".

This tells you to
look for and think about
ways to bless others.

Life will become
exciting when you do!

BIBLICAL BASIS

"He that is faithful in that which is least is faithful also in much; and he that is unjust in the least is unjust also in much."

Luke 16:10 KJV

MENTOR MESSAGE

WHAT'S NEXT IN YOUR LIFE IS DETERMINED BY WHAT'S NOW IN YOUR LIFE.

HE THAT IS FAITHFUL IN THAT WHICH IS FAITHFUL IN MUCH

SON STANDARD

Your faithfulness today qualifies you for a better tomorrow.

Your unfaithfulness today disqualifies you for a better tomorrow.

BIBLICAL BASIS

"Be sober, be vigilant; because your adversary the devil walks about like a roaring lion, seeking whom he may devour."   - I Peter 5:8

MENTOR MESSAGE

IF THE DEVIL CAN'T MAKE YOU BAD, HE'LL MAKE YOU BUSY. IF THE DEVIL CAN'T DESTROY YOU HE WILL TRY TO DISTRACT YOU!

SON STANDARD

The devil is known as Beelzebub. This means "lord of the flies". Flies won't kill you but they will distract you!

BIBLICAL BASIS

"For he who would love life and see good days, let him refrain his tongue from evil, and his lips from speaking deceit."

— 1 Peter 3:10

MENTOR MESSAGE

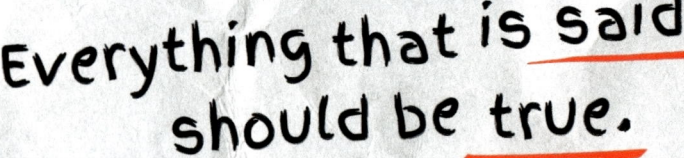

Everything that is said should be true.

Not everything true should be said.

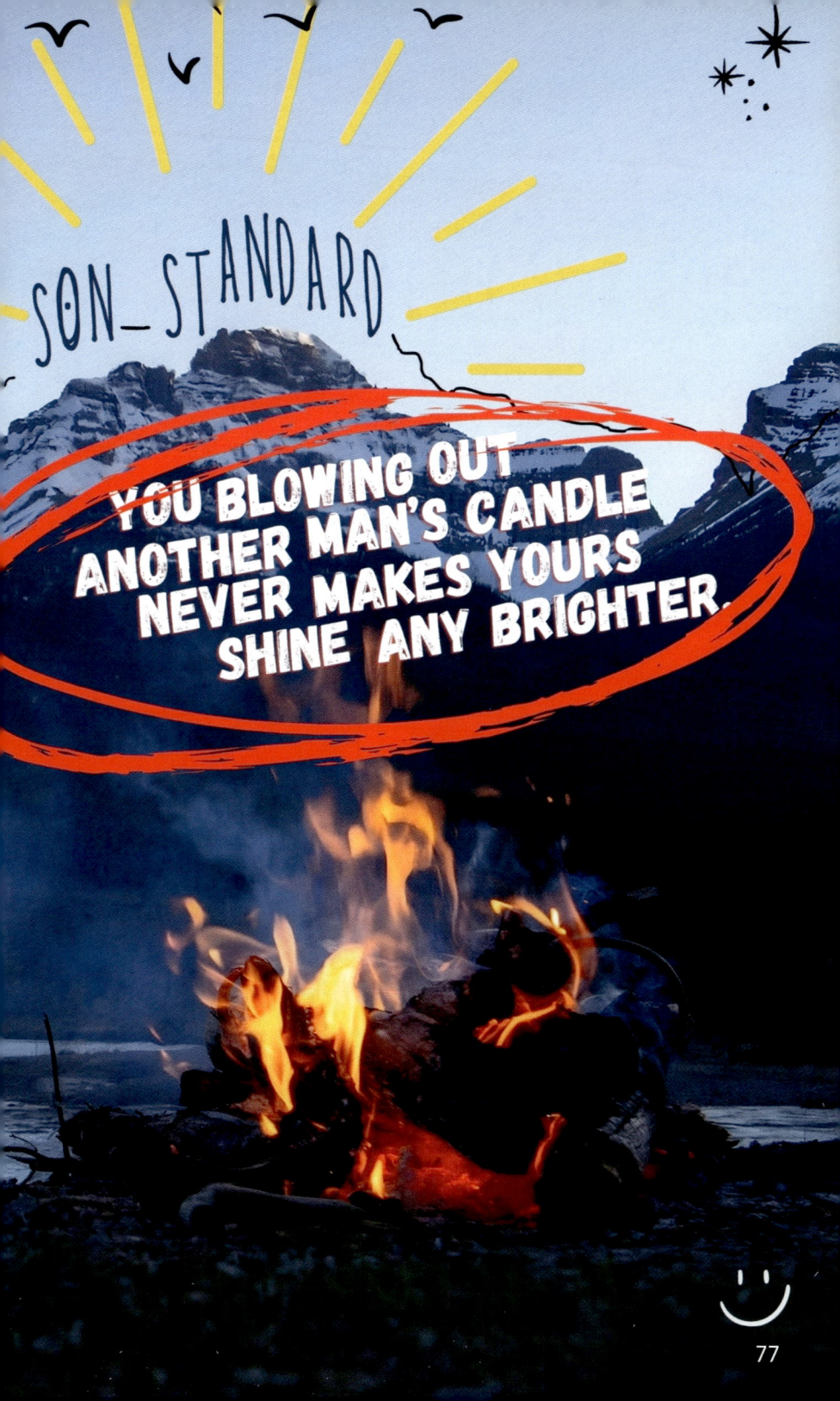

WEEK 34

BIBLICAL BASIS

"FOR WE MUST ALL APPEAR BEFORE THE JUDGMENT SEAT OF CHRIST, THAT EACH ONE MAY RECEIVE THE THINGS DONE IN THE BODY, ACCORDING TO WHAT HE HAS DONE, WHETHER GOOD OR BAD."

2 CORINTHIANS 5:10

MENTOR MESSAGE

THERE'S A DIFFERENCE BETWEEN BELIEF AND BEHAVIOR.

BELIEF DETERMINES WHERE YOU SPEND ETERNITY.

BEHAVIOR DETERMINES HOW YOU SPEND ETERNITY.

SON STANDARD

IT IS GRACE AND FAITH ALONE THAT DETERMINES YOUR SALVATION. HOWEVER, WHAT YOU DO ON EARTH IN HIS NAME WILL DETERMINE YOUR REWARDS.

WEEK 35

"THESE PEOPLE DRAW NEAR TO ME WITH THEIR MOUTH, AND HONOR ME WITH THEIR LIPS, BUT THEIR HEART IS FAR FROM ME."

MATTHEW 15:8

MENTOR MESSAGE

WORSHIP IS NOT JUST THE SONG YOU SING. WORSHIP IS THE LIFE YOU LIVE.

SON STANDARD

LEARN TO MATCH YOUR LIPS WITH YOUR LIFE.

PERFECTION IS NOT REQUIRED... CONSISTENCY IS.

35

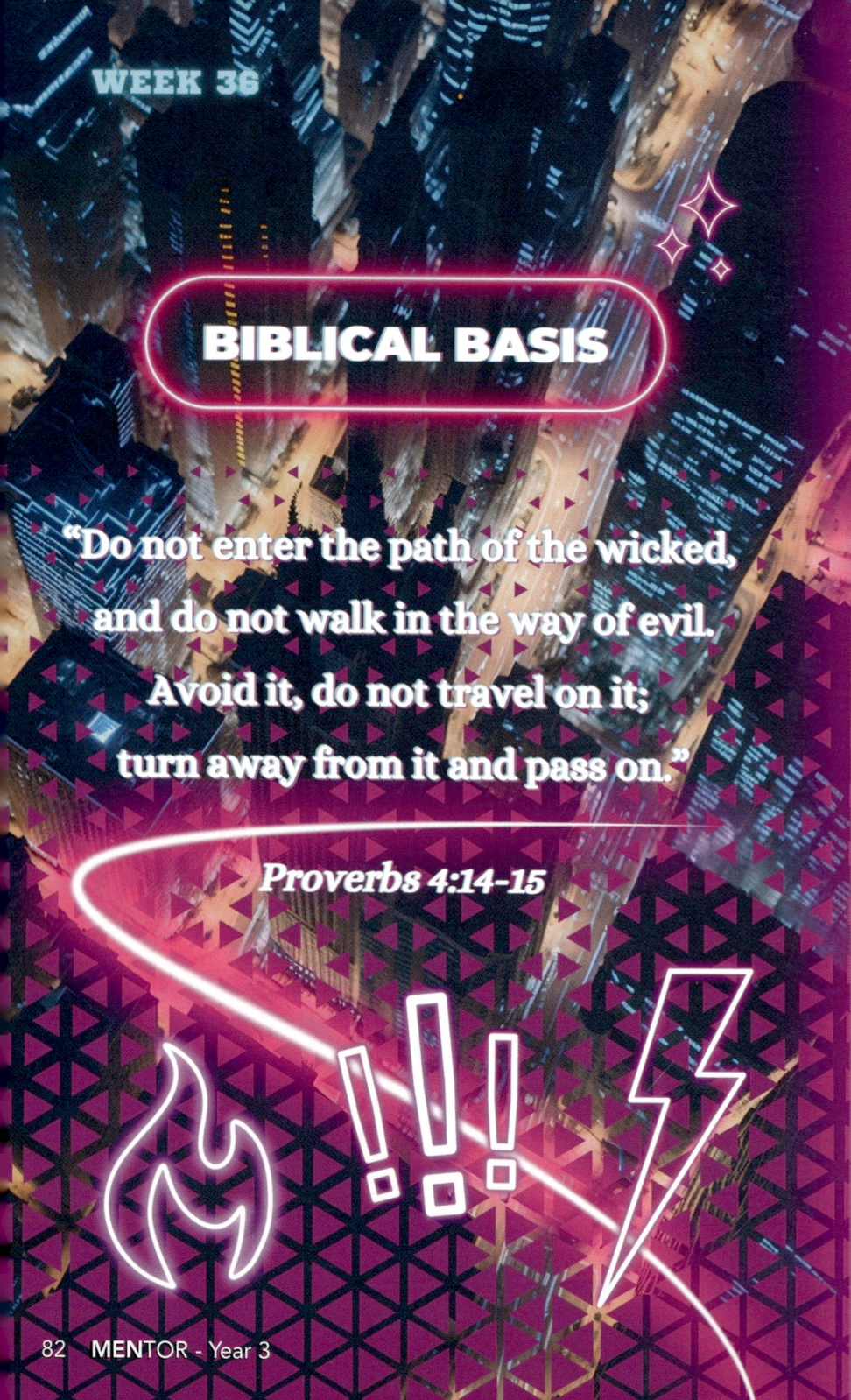

BIBLICAL BASIS

"Do not enter the path of the wicked,
and do not walk in the way of evil.
Avoid it, do not travel on it;
turn away from it and pass on."

Proverbs 4:14-15

MENTOR MESSAGE

Life is not about intention,
it is about prevention.

The best of intentions
can go awry with
the worst of positions.

SON STANDARD

We all intend to do
the right things.

However, being alone
with a girl at 3:00 in
the morning studying
the Song of Solomon
does not put you in
a very good position!

BIBLICAL BASIS

"THE HORSE IS PREPARED FOR THE DAY OF BATTLE, BUT DELIVERANCE IS OF THE LORD."
- PROVERBS 21:31

MENTOR MESSAGE

PREPARATION TIME IS NEVER Wasted Time

YOU MUST
PREPARE FOR

WHAT GOD
HAS PREPARED
FOR YOU

BIBLICAL BASIS

"But I want you to be without care. He who is unmarried cares for the things of the Lord – how he may please the Lord . . ."

"And this I say for your own profit, not that I may put a leash on you, but for what is proper, and that you may serve the Lord without distraction."

– I Corinthians 7:32, 35

MENTOR MESSAGE

Learn the difference between:

- Attractive and attracted
- Alone and lonely
- Emotion and emotional

Being single is not a disease!

It is a period of time in which you can set Godly priorities. You are complete in Him!

BIBLICAL BASIS

"Whereas you do not know what will happen tomorrow. For what is your life? It is even a vapor that appears for a little time and then vanishes away."
- James 4:14

MENTOR MESSAGE

Life is short...make it count.

Life is long...pace yourself.

SON STANDARD

Learn to **BALANCE** these Biblical principles and you will neither

Burn out for God or
Rust out for the devil!

LIFE

MAKE IT
COUNT

Biblical Basis

"And he said to them,
'Take heed and beware of covetousness,
for one's life does not consist in the
abundance of the things he possesses.'"

– Luke 12:15

Mentor Message

*Money can add
meaning to your life,
but money is not
the meaning of life.*

Son Standard

Quality of life is always more important
than standard of living.

Biblical Basis

"But seek first the kingdom of God and His righteousness, and all these things shall be added to you."

MATTHEW 6:33

MENTOR Message

Service over status.

Character over convenience.

Holiness over happiness.

Purpose over popularity.

Availability over ability.

We over me.

son standard

Choose first
what truly matters!

BIBLICAL BASIS

"AND BE RENEWED IN THE SPIRIT OF YOUR MIND"
- EPHESIANS 4:23

MENTOR MESSAGE

You can't change the culture if you are the same as the culture.

Put yourself in their shoes . . . don't put yourself in their sin.

SON STANDARD

SOMETIMES THE CHURCH IS SO WORLDLY
AND THE WORLD IS SO CHURCHY. . .
YOU CAN'T TELL THE DIFFERENCE!

95

BIBLICAL BASIS

"But as for me,
I will walk in my integrity;"
- Psalms 26:11a

MENTOR MESSAGE

SUCCESSFUL
PEOPLE MAKE
RIGHT DECISIONS
IN THE MIDST OF
WRONG FEELINGS.

SUCCESSFUL
PEOPLE MAKE
POSITIVE DECISIONS
IN THE MIDST OF
NEGATIVE
CIRCUMSTANCES.

SON STANDARD

WHEN YOU HAVE MUD ON YOUR SHOES, DON'T KEEP WALKING ON WHITE CARPET ...

IT ONLY COMPOUNDS THE MESS

BIBLICAL BASIS

"SO THEN, MY BELOVED BRETHREN,
LET EVERY MAN BE SWIFT TO HEAR,
SLOW TO SPEAK, SLOW TO WRATH;"
- JAMES 1:19

MENTOR MESSAGE

IT ALWAYS TAKES TIME TO ACCESS YOUR WISER SELF.

SON

STANDARD

Think before
you speak.

Take a day
before you post.

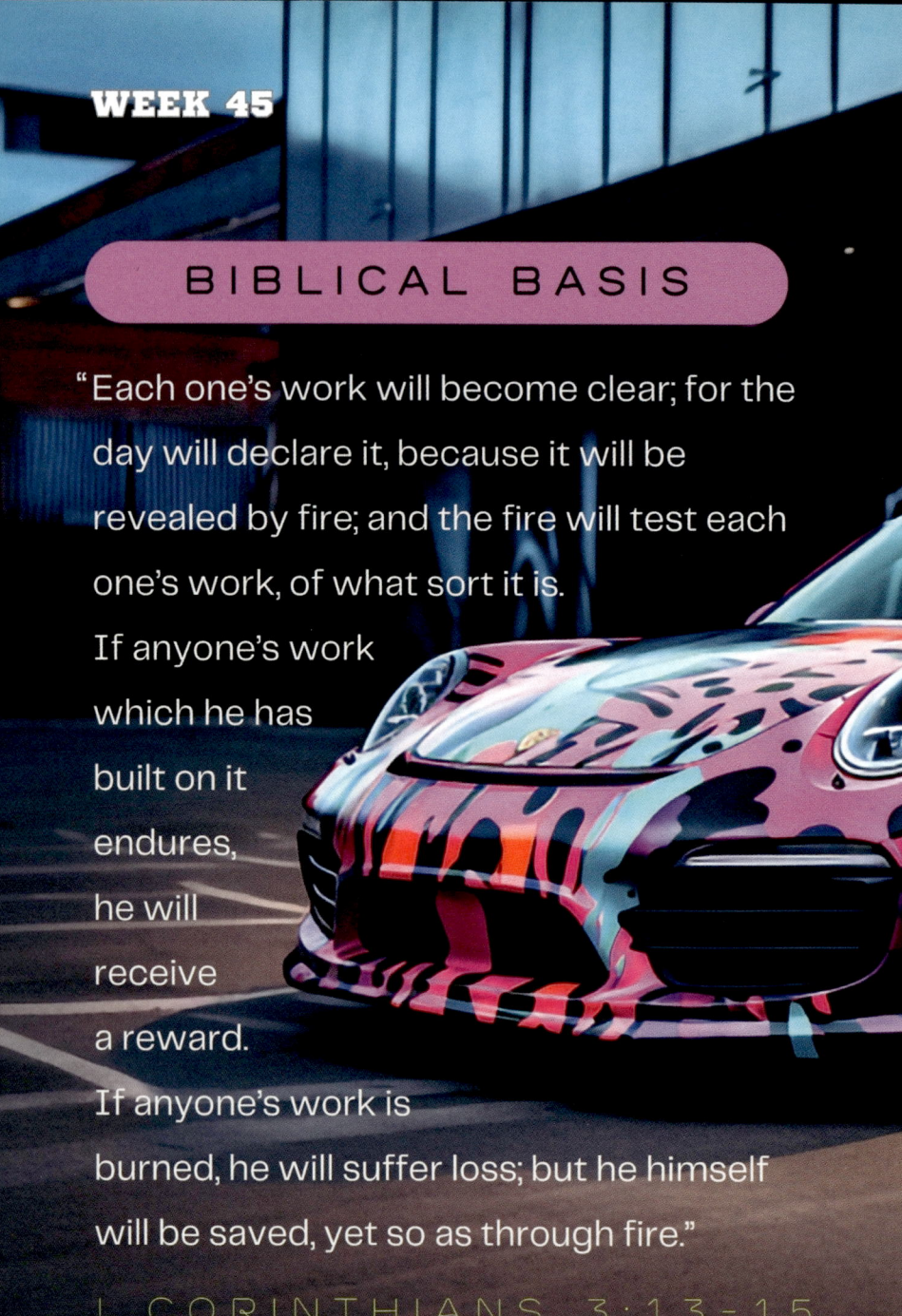

BIBLICAL BASIS

"Each one's work will become clear; for the day will declare it, because it will be revealed by fire; and the fire will test each one's work, of what sort it is. If anyone's work which he has built on it endures, he will receive a reward. If anyone's work is burned, he will suffer loss; but he himself will be saved, yet so as through fire."

I CORINTHIANS 3:13-15

The worst thing you can do is not failure . . . the worst thing you can do is succeed at something that doesn't matter!

SON STANDARD

Make sure what you give your life to matters for eternity!

BIBLICAL BASIS

"DO NOT BE OVERCOME BY EVIL, BUT OVERCOME EVIL WITH GOOD."

- Romans 12:21

MENTOR MESSAGE

THE END DOESN'T JUSTIFY THE MEANS. IF WE TAKE CARE OF OUR "MEANS" TODAY, GOD WILL TAKE CARE OF THE "END" TOMORROW.

SON STANDARD

YOU CAN NEVER COMPROMISE YOUR WAY TO SUCESS!

biblical basis

"Therefore
submit to God.
Resist the devil
and he will
flee from you."

– James 4:7

mentor message

YOUR AUTHORITY OVER THE DEVIL WILL NEVER RISE ABOVE YOUR RELATIONSHIP WITH GOD.

son standard

IF YOUR RESISTER ISN'T WORKING... CHECK YOUR SUBMITTER!

BIBLICAL BASIS

"Then He said to them, 'Follow me and I will make you fishers of men.'"
– *Matthew 4:19*

MENTOR MESSAGE

The problem with always doing what **you** want to do is that you might end up **somewhere** you don't want to be.

SON STANDARD

FOLLOW HIM!

HIS THERE IS ALWAYS BETTER THAN YOUR HERE!

biblical basis

"FOR WE DARE NOT CLASS OURSELVES OR COMPARE OURSELVES WITH THOSE WHO COMMEND THEMSELVES. BUT THEY, MEASURING THEMSELVES BY THEMSELVES, AND COMPARING THEMSELVES AMONG THEMSELVES, ARE NOT WISE."

2 CORINTHIANS 10:12

mentor message

I'D RATHER YOU BE A GREAT YOU THAN A POOR ME. THE EASIEST PERSON IN THE WORLD TO BE...IS YOU!

son standard

GOD CANNOT BLESS THOSE WHO WE PRETEND TO BE.

WEEK 50

BIBLICAL BASIS

"If any of you lacks wisdom, let him ask of God, who gives to all liberally and without reproach, and it will be given to him."
- *James 1:5*

MENTOR MESSAGE

When we change the way we look at things...
THE THINGS WE LOOK AT CHANGE.

SON STANDARD

PERSPECTIVE IS EVERYTHING!

A LEADER'S NUMBER ONE JOB IS TO **GET** AND **GIVE** PERSPECTIVE.

BIBLICAL BASIS

"BUT BY THE GRACE OF GOD I AM WHAT I AM, AND HIS GRACE TOWARD ME WAS NOT IN VAIN; BUT I LABORED MORE ABUNDANTLY THAN THEY ALL, YET NOT I, BUT THE GRACE OF GOD WHICH WAS WITH ME."

- 1 Corinthians 15:10

MENTOR MESSAGE

THE VALUE OF A MAN'S LIFE IS MEASURED BY HOW MUCH OF IT HE GIVES AWAY.

SON STANDARD

POURING YOUR LIFE OUT IS THE BEST WAY TO FILL IT UP.

BIBLICAL
Basis

"looking unto Jesus, the author and finisher of our faith, who for the joy that was set before Him endured the cross, despising the shame, and has sat down at the right hand of the throne of God."

HEBREWS 12:2

💬 MENTOR MESSAGE   now

The cross is proof that Jesus would rather die for you than to live without you.

GOD
LOVES
YOU

as if you are
the only person
in this world to love!

The End beginning

HOW TO START THE MOST IMPORTANT RELATIONSHIP OF YOUR LIFE

Shark fishing is my hobby. I use a kayak to paddle my bait hundreds of yards into the ocean, then paddle back and fish from the shore. Some time ago, I was in the middle of a four-hour battle with a very large shark, and a crowd had gathered from around the beach to see what I was going to reel in! A man in the crowd struck up a conversation with me while I was battling this shark. He asked me what I did for a living, and I told him I was a pastor.

When people discover that I am a pastor, I get a variety of responses. This man's response was unusual. He simply blurted out with disdain, "Well, I hate organized religion!" I replied, "Me too." He was surprised at my reply, so I continued, asking, "Do you know who else hates organized religion?" Before he could respond, I shocked him further and said, "Jesus!" Now, I had this fellow's undivided attention, and I hope that I now have yours as well.

You see, Christianity is not about religion. It is about a relationship with a loving, heavenly Father through His one Son, Jesus Christ.

I believe that you have a figurative homing beacon on the inside of you, placed there by the God who created you. It is a spiritual hole, if you will, that can only be filled by God.

I understand this personally. Before I entered into a relationship with Jesus, I tried to fill that hole with women, alcohol, and fighting. It was fun for a while, but when the fun was over and the things I tried to fill that vacuum with came crashing down around me, I still had that homing beacon on the inside of me. It was my heavenly Father, gently, patiently, and ever so lovingly, calling me home.

Maybe you can sense the emptiness on the inside of you and the loving call of your heavenly Father, imploring you to come home. Why not surrender your life to Him and find the joy, peace, and purpose you've been looking for all your life? Why not start the most important relationship of your life? It's so simple, but life transforming.

Please pray this prayer with me. Repeat it out loud, but mean it from your heart. I discovered a long time ago that when you reach out to God from your heart, He will always reach back to you with His love.

Pray this simple prayer with me now:

> "Father God, I come to you now. Sin, I turn my back on you. Jesus, I turn to You now. I believe you were raised from the dead just for me. Come into my heart, and be my LORD. I surrender my life to you today. I enter into a relationship with you today!"

If you prayed that prayer, please contact us here at Joy Church and let us know that you started the most important relationship of your life. We want to respect your privacy and dignity, but we also want to give you some information to help you walk out this new relationship in a life-giving way!

You can email us at mail@joychurch.net or give us a call at 615-773-5252. You can also write to us at Joy Church, P.O. Box 247, Mount Juliet, TN, 37121.

If you live in or are visiting the Nashville/Mount Juliet, TN area, we would love to invite you to join us for one of our upcoming services. For more information and directions, please visit our website at joychurch.net. We look forward to hearing from you!

Please remember that God loves you as if you were the only person in this world to love!

Jim Frease and his wife, Anne, and their son, Johnathan.

ABOUT THE AUTHOR

Jim Frease is the founder and senior pastor of Joy Church in Mt. Juliet, Tennessee, and founder and president of World Changers Bible Institute.

He is also the founder of Joy Ministerial Exchange, a ministerial organization designed to impart to pastors from across the country.

Jim emphasizes a relationship with Jesus Christ, not religion; the Word of God, not tradition; and enjoying life, not enduring it. He teaches not just what to do, but how.

Jim and his wife, Anne, have been married since 1990, and they deeply love their son, Johnathan. Jim loves spending time with his family, and he enjoys Ohio State football and fishing. Anne loves to shop. Sometimes, they compromise and shop at Bass Pro Shops®.

Most importantly, Jim and Anne are deeply in love with the Lord Jesus Christ and are completely committed to His Word. As they minister, they do so with humor & joy (Nehemiah 8:10) and integrity (Psalm 26:11), propelling the listener to a greater intimacy with Jesus.

ABOUT JOY CHURCH

Based out of Mt. Juliet, Tennessee,
Joy Church is a rapidly growing, multigenerational,
multicultural church with people from almost every
denominational background—including those with
no church background at all.

At Joy Church, we don't believe in organized religion.
We believe in an organized relationship with
God the Father through His Son, Jesus Christ.

We are not about tradition
but the liberating Word of God.

We are not about enduring life.
We are about enjoying life!

For more information, please visit joychurch.net